# MOTORCYCLES

Written by Caitlin Fraser

Flying Start to Literacy®

# Contents

# Introduction

Many people ride motorcycles.

Motorcycles can go where cars cannot go. They can take off and they can turn quickly.

They can race over jumps and
fly high into the air.

These things make motorcycles great
for work and for sports.

# Motorcycles at work

Some people ride motorcycles when they are working.

## Police motorcycles

The police use motorcycles. Motorcycles can go fast and they can move between cars.

Police use motorcycles to keep our roads safe. They make sure drivers obey the road rules. And police use motorcycles to get to people quickly in an emergency.

## Motorcycles on farms

In some parts of the world, farmers
ride motorcycles. Farmers on large farms
use motorcycles to get to all parts of
their farms.

Motorcycles can go where there are no roads. They can go up and down hills and over the muddy ground.

# Motorcycle sports

Some people ride motorcycles as a sport.

## Motorcycle racing

Some people race motorcycles. They ride as fast as they can around a track. The winner is the rider who finishes the race first.

## Freestyle motocross

In this sport, the track has many turns and jumps. Each rider gets points for doing jumps and stunts. The winner is the rider who gets the most points.

# Hill climb

Hill climb is a sport where riders race up very steep hills. The first rider to get to the top of the hill is the winner. If no rider makes it to the top of the hill, then the rider who gets closest to the top wins.

# Motoball

In some countries, people play ball sports on motorcycles. Motoball is like soccer, but the players ride motorcycles. They play with a ball that is twice as big as a soccer ball.

Players try to get the ball into the goal, which is a large net. They can kick the ball or hit it with their heads. They cannot touch the ball with their hands.

# Chapter 3 Motorcycle stunts

Some motorcycle riders put on shows where they do amazing stunts.

## The Ball of Death

The Ball of Death is a large metal ball.
A motorcycle rider rides around inside
the ball doing stunts. Sometimes there
is more than one rider inside the ball.

# Motorcycle jumps

At some motorcycle shows, riders do amazing jumps. They ride up a big ramp and jump over cars, buses or trucks.

Some riders do stunts on their motorcycles while they are in the air.

# Chapter 4

# Motorcycle safety

Motorcycle riders wear clothes that help to keep their bodies safe.

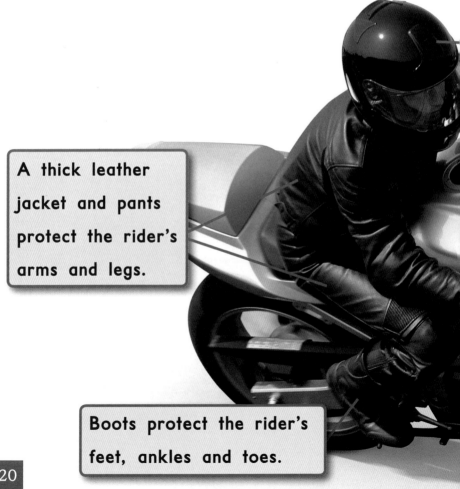

A thick leather jacket and pants protect the rider's arms and legs.

Boots protect the rider's feet, ankles and toes.

It can be very dangerous if a motorcycle rider falls off the motorcycle or is hit by a car.

A helmet protects the rider's head.

Gloves protect the rider's hands.

# Conclusion

People ride motorcycles for many different reasons. They ride them for work, for fun and sport, and to entertain people.

## Work

# Fun and sport

# Entertainment

23

# Index